Constitution Of An Independent Scotland

By James Hosie

1

Preamble:

We, the people of Scotland, in recognition of our shared history, diverse identities, and the inherent dignity of every individual, hereby establish this constitution to guide our journey as an independent and progressive nation.

Mindful of the principles of democracy, justice,

and equality, we affirm our commitment to building a society that cherishes freedom, respects human rights, and embraces the values of inclusivity and diversity.

As custodians of Scotland's rich cultural heritage and stewards of its natural beauty, we pledge to create a nation that not only safeguards its past but also nurtures a sustainable and

harmonious future
for generations to
come.

In the spirit of
cooperation and
goodwill, we
extend our hand to
the global
community,
aspiring to

contribute to the world's progress while cherishing our distinct national identity.

With this constitution, we lay the foundation for a Scotland that thrives on the principles of fairness, compassion, and progress. May this document serve as a beacon, guiding us toward a future where every citizen can flourish, and the collective aspirations of our

people find
fulfillment.

2

Fundamental Rights and Freedoms:

In recognition of
the inherent dignity

and equal rights of all individuals, this constitution enshrines a comprehensive set of fundamental rights and freedoms as the bedrock of our society.

Right to Life:

Every person has the inherent right to life, and the state shall protect this right, promoting policies that ensure the well-being and health of all citizens.

Equality before the Law: All individuals are equal before the law, and discrimination on the basis of race, gender, religion, ethnicity, sexual orientation, or any other grounds is prohibited.

Freedom of Expression: The right to freedom of expression is upheld, fostering a vibrant public discourse that encourages diverse

opinions and
perspectives.

Right to Privacy:
The privacy of
individuals is
inviolable, and the
state shall protect
against
unwarranted
intrusion, ensuring

the security and autonomy of personal information.

Freedom of Assembly and Association: Citizens have the right to peacefully assemble and associate, contributing to the flourishing of civil society and participatory democracy.

Right to Education: Every person has the right to accessible and quality education, promoting lifelong learning, critical thinking, and the pursuit of knowledge.

Freedom of Religion and Belief: The right to freedom of

thought, conscience, and religion is respected, ensuring that individuals can practice their beliefs without fear of persecution.

Right to a Fair Trial: The right to a

fair and impartial
trial is guaranteed,
upholding the
principles of
justice, due
process, and the
rule of law.

Protection from
Torture and
Inhuman

Treatment: All individuals shall be protected from torture, cruel, or inhuman treatment, with the state committed to preventing and redressing such acts.

Right to Participate in Government:

Citizens have the right to participate in the democratic process, including the right to vote and stand for public office, ensuring the legitimacy and accountability of government institutions.

3

Democratic Governance:

In fostering a robust and

participatory democracy, this constitution outlines the principles and mechanisms for the governance of our independent nation.

Separation of Powers: The

powers of the state shall be divided among the executive, legislative, and judicial branches, ensuring a system of checks and balances to prevent the abuse of authority.

Elections and
Representation:
Regular, free, and
fair elections shall
be held, allowing
citizens to choose
their
representatives and
ensuring the
accountability of

those in public office.

Proportional Representation: The electoral system shall be designed to promote proportional representation, reflecting the diversity of the population and encouraging the inclusion of varied voices in the political landscape.

Citizen Participation: Mechanisms for

direct citizen participation in decision-making processes shall be established, fostering engagement and empowering citizens to contribute to the development of policies that affect their lives.

Transparent Government: The government shall operate with transparency, providing access to information and ensuring openness

in its actions,
thereby building
trust between the
state and its
citizens.

Local Governance:
Devolution of
powers to local
governments and
communities shall

be promoted, allowing for tailored approaches to regional needs and encouraging local participation in decision-making.

Protection of Minority Rights:

Safeguards shall be in place to protect the rights of minorities, ensuring their full and equal participation in the political, social, and cultural life of the nation.

Rule of Law: The rule of law shall be paramount, with legal mechanisms in place to uphold justice, protect individual rights, and prevent arbitrary exercise of power.

Emergency
Powers: Provisions
for the declaration
of a state of
emergency shall be
clearly defined,
with safeguards to
prevent the abuse
of such powers and
the protection of
essential

democratic principles even in times of crisis.

Public Service Ethics: Public officials shall adhere to the highest standards of ethical conduct, promoting integrity, accountability, and responsibility in the service of the public.

4

Environmental Stewardship:

Recognizing the interconnectedness of our well-being with the health of our environment, this constitution underscores the commitment of an independent Scotland to environmental sustainability and stewardship.

Right to a Healthy Environment: Every citizen has the right to live in an environment that supports their well-being, and the state shall take measures to protect and enhance the quality of air, water, and ecosystems.

Sustainable Development: Policies and practices shall be guided by the principles of sustainable development, balancing economic growth with environmental conservation to ensure a resilient and thriving nation for future generations.

Biodiversity Conservation: The state shall actively work to preserve and enhance biodiversity, recognizing the intrinsic value of diverse ecosystems and the critical role

they play in
maintaining
ecological balance.

Climate Action:
Scotland commits
to ambitious and
responsible climate
action, aiming to
reduce carbon
emissions,

transition to renewable energy sources, and contribute to global efforts to address climate change.

Responsible Resource Management: Natural resources

shall be managed responsibly, minimizing waste, promoting recycling, and ensuring equitable access to resources while preventing overexploitation.

Environmental Education: The importance of environmental education shall be emphasized, fostering a culture of environmental awareness and responsibility

among citizens
from an early age.

Access to Nature:
Efforts shall be
made to ensure that
all citizens have
equitable access to
natural spaces,
promoting the
physical and

mental health benefits of connecting with the natural environment.

Environmental Justice: Environmental policies shall be designed to avoid disproportionate impacts on marginalized communities, ensuring that the benefits and burdens of environmental decisions are distributed fairly.

International Cooperation on Environmental Issues: Scotland shall actively engage in international cooperation to address global environmental challenges, recognizing the shared responsibility to protect the planet for current and future generations.

Innovation for Sustainability: Encouragement and support for innovation in sustainable practices and technologies shall be a priority, fostering a culture of continuous improvement in environmental stewardship.

5

Social Justice:

Emphasizing the pursuit of fairness and equity, this section outlines the principles that guide the commitment of an

independent
Scotland to social
justice for all its
citizens.

Eradication of
Discrimination:
The state shall
actively work to
eliminate all forms
of discrimination,

including but not limited to, those based on race, gender, sexual orientation, disability, and socioeconomic status.

Equality of Opportunity:

Policies shall be implemented to ensure equal opportunities for all citizens, irrespective of background, fostering an inclusive society that values the diverse talents and contributions of its people.

Poverty Alleviation: A commitment to reducing and ultimately eliminating poverty through targeted social programs, economic empowerment, and the creation of an inclusive economic environment.

Access to Healthcare: Universal access to comprehensive healthcare services shall be guaranteed, recognizing health as a fundamental right and addressing health disparities to ensure the well-being of all citizens.

Housing as a Right: The state shall work towards ensuring affordable and adequate housing for all citizens, recognizing the importance of stable housing as a foundation for individual and community well-being.

Quality Education for All: Equal access to quality education shall be ensured, with initiatives to address disparities in educational outcomes and opportunities, promoting a society where every individual can reach their full potential.

Criminal Justice Reform: A

commitment to a fair and rehabilitative criminal justice system, with a focus on addressing the root causes of crime, reducing recidivism, and ensuring justice is administered impartially.

Inclusive Economic Growth: Economic policies shall aim for inclusive growth, creating opportunities for all citizens to participate in and benefit from the nation's prosperity, with a particular focus on narrowing income inequality.

Social Safety Nets: Robust social safety nets shall be established to provide support for those facing economic hardships, ensuring that no citizen is left without the means to meet their basic needs.

Community Engagement:

Encouragement of community-driven initiatives and participatory decision-making processes, empowering local communities to actively contribute to shaping policies

that impact their
well-being.

6

Cultural Heritage
and Diversity:

Affirming the rich
tapestry of
Scotland's cultural

identity, this section emphasizes the importance of preserving, celebrating, and embracing cultural diversity as a source of strength and unity.

Recognition of Cultural Diversity:

Scotland recognizes and celebrates the diverse cultural identities, languages, and traditions that contribute to the nation's unique heritage.

Protection of Linguistic Diversity: Measures shall be taken to protect and promote linguistic diversity, recognizing the importance of preserving and revitalizing minority languages alongside the national language(s).

Cultural Preservation: The state shall support

initiatives to preserve and promote historical sites, artifacts, and cultural practices, ensuring that the legacy of Scotland's past is passed down to future generations.

Inclusive Cultural Policies: Cultural policies shall be inclusive, fostering opportunities for artists, creators, and cultural practitioners from all backgrounds to contribute to the nation's cultural landscape.

Education in Cultural Heritage: Educational curricula shall include the study and appreciation of Scotland's cultural heritage, instilling a sense of pride and connection to the nation's history and traditions.

Promotion of the Arts: The state shall encourage and support the arts in all their forms, recognizing their role in reflecting and shaping the cultural identity of the nation.

Intercultural Dialogue: Initiatives promoting intercultural dialogue and understanding shall be fostered, creating spaces for different communities to engage and learn from one another.

Protection of Indigenous Rights: Special attention

shall be given to
the protection of
the rights and
interests of
indigenous
communities,
acknowledging
their unique
contributions to
Scotland's cultural

and historical
fabric.

Freedom of
Cultural
Expression: Every
citizen shall have
the right to freely
express, practice,
and share their
cultural identity

without fear of discrimination or marginalization.

Cultural Exchange: Encouragement of cultural exchange programs, both domestically and internationally, to strengthen

connections
between different
communities and
promote a global
appreciation of
Scotland's cultural
richness.

7

Education for All:

Recognizing the transformative power of education, this section outlines the principles that guide the commitment of an independent Scotland to

providing
accessible and
quality education
for all its citizens.

Right to Education:
Education is
declared a
fundamental right,
and the state shall
ensure that every

citizen has access to free, compulsory, and quality education at all levels.

Inclusive Education: Policies shall be enacted to promote inclusive education, accommodating diverse learning needs and ensuring that no one is excluded from educational opportunities based on any form of discrimination.

Early Childhood Education:

Recognizing the importance of early childhood development, efforts shall be made to provide accessible and high-quality early childhood education, setting the foundation for lifelong learning.

Equal Opportunities in Higher Education: Equal opportunities for access to higher education shall be guaranteed, with measures to address disparities and ensure that individuals from all backgrounds have the chance to pursue advanced studies.

Promotion of Critical Thinking:

The education system shall emphasize the development of critical thinking skills, creativity, and a spirit of inquiry, preparing students to engage meaningfully in a rapidly evolving world.

Digital Literacy: Given the importance of technology, efforts shall be made to integrate digital literacy into the education curriculum, equipping students with the skills necessary for the digital age.

Civic Education: Civic education shall be promoted to instill an understanding of democratic principles, social responsibility, and active citizenship, fostering an engaged and informed citizenry.

Teacher Training and Professional Development:

Continuous investment in teacher training and professional development programs shall be prioritized, ensuring that educators are well-equipped to provide quality and

up-to-date
instruction.

Languages and
Multicultural
Education:
Recognition of the
importance of
multilingualism
and multicultural
education,

promoting linguistic diversity and intercultural understanding within the education system.

Lifelong Learning Opportunities: A commitment to providing

opportunities for lifelong learning, with initiatives to support ongoing education and skill development for individuals at all stages of life.

8

Health and Well-being:

Prioritizing the health and well-being of its citizens, this section outlines the principles that guide the commitment of an

independent
Scotland to
ensuring accessible
and comprehensive
healthcare services
for all.

Right to Health:
The right to the
highest attainable
standard of

physical and mental health is affirmed as a fundamental right, and the state shall work to ensure the well-being of all citizens.

Universal Healthcare: A

commitment to a universal healthcare system, where all citizens have equal access to essential healthcare services without discrimination, ensuring no one is left behind.

Preventive Healthcare: Policies shall prioritize preventive healthcare measures, promoting awareness, screenings, and vaccinations to reduce the incidence of diseases and improve overall public health.

Mental Health Support: Recognition of mental health as an

integral component of overall well-being, with policies to destigmatize mental health issues and ensure access to quality mental health services.

Primary Healthcare: Strengthening primary healthcare services to provide accessible and comprehensive care at the community level, addressing health

needs efficiently
and proactively.

Health Equity:
Efforts shall be
made to address
health disparities
and inequalities,
ensuring that
vulnerable and
marginalized

populations receive adequate healthcare services and attention.

Patient Rights: Protection of patient rights, including the right to informed consent, confidentiality, and dignified treatment, with mechanisms for addressing grievances and ensuring accountability within the healthcare system.

Medical Research and Innovation: Support for medical research and innovation to advance healthcare practices, treatments, and technologies, contributing to the improvement of

overall public health.

Public Health Initiatives: Implementation of public health initiatives addressing issues such as nutrition, sanitation, and lifestyle choices to promote a holistic approach to well-being.

Emergency Preparedness: Establishment of robust emergency preparedness and response systems to address health crises, ensuring the protection of citizens in times of pandemics, natural disasters, or other emergencies.

9

Economic Prosperity and Social Welfare:

Focusing on the economic foundations of the nation, this section outlines the principles that guide the commitment of an independent Scotland to fostering economic prosperity and social welfare for all its citizens.

Inclusive Economic Growth: Economic policies

shall be designed to promote inclusive and sustainable economic growth, creating opportunities for prosperity that benefit all citizens.

Employment Rights: Protection

and enhancement of workers' rights, ensuring fair wages, safe working conditions, and the right to organize, fostering a balanced and equitable workplace environment.

Social Safety Nets: Establishment and maintenance of robust social safety nets to provide support for those facing unemployment, disability, or other economic hardships, ensuring a basic standard of living for all citizens.

Affordable Housing: Policies shall be implemented to

ensure the availability of affordable and quality housing, recognizing the importance of stable housing as a key component of social welfare.

Access to Financial Services: Efforts to promote financial inclusion, providing access to affordable banking and financial services for all citizens, fostering economic independence and resilience.

Education and Skills Development: Investment in education and skills development programs to empower citizens with the tools necessary to adapt and thrive in a rapidly evolving economic landscape.

Environmental Sustainability in Economics: Integration of

environmental sustainability principles into economic policies, recognizing the importance of responsible resource management and reducing the environmental impact of economic activities.

Innovation and Technology: Encouragement of innovation and the adoption of technology to drive economic development, with a focus on creating a dynamic and competitive economy.

Support for Small and Medium Enterprises (SMEs): Policies shall be enacted to support the growth of SMEs, recognizing their role as engines of economic development and sources of employment.

International Trade and Cooperation:

Active engagement in international trade and cooperation, fostering economic partnerships that contribute to the prosperity of the nation and its citizens.

10

International Cooperation:

Acknowledging the interconnectedness of the global community, this section outlines the

principles guiding
the commitment of
an independent
Scotland to
constructive and
collaborative
international
relations.

Peaceful Relations:
A commitment to

peaceful and diplomatic solutions to conflicts, promoting dialogue and negotiation as fundamental tools for resolving international disputes.

Respect for
International Law:
Adherence to
international law
and treaties,
recognizing their
importance in
maintaining global
order, promoting
justice, and
ensuring the

protection of
human rights.

Human Rights
Advocacy: Active
participation in
international
forums to advocate
for the promotion
and protection of
human rights

globally, contributing to a world where dignity and equality are universal principles.

Global Health Initiatives: Participation in

global health initiatives, contributing resources and expertise to address global health challenges, including pandemics and public health emergencies.

Environmental Stewardship on the Global Stage: A commitment to international efforts to address climate change, protect biodiversity, and promote sustainable

development, recognizing the shared responsibility to safeguard the planet.

Aid and Development Assistance: Participation in

international development efforts, providing aid and assistance to less developed nations, with a focus on poverty alleviation, education, and healthcare.

Cultural Exchange Programs: Promotion of cultural exchange programs to enhance understanding and appreciation between nations, fostering mutual respect and

celebrating the diversity of global cultures.

Refugee Protection: Commitment to protecting the rights of refugees and displaced persons, supporting international efforts to provide humanitarian assistance and find durable solutions to forced displacement.

Peacekeeping and Conflict Resolution:

Willingness to contribute to international peacekeeping efforts and conflict resolution initiatives, working collaboratively to prevent and address conflicts around the world.

Promotion of
Global
Cooperation:
Active engagement
in international
organizations and
forums, promoting
multilateralism and
collective action to
address global

challenges and build a more just and equitable world.

www.ingramcontent.com/pod-product-compliance
Lightning Source LLC
Chambersburg PA
CBHW070949260726
48661CB00003B/1204